LAST OF A BREED

LAST OF

A BREED

Portraits of Working Cowboys

MARTIN H. SCHREIBER

BANTAM BOOKS

TORONTO • NEW YORK • LONDON • SYDNEY • AUCKLAND

LAST OF A BREED:
PORTRAITS OF WORKING COWBOYS
A Bantam Book/published by arrangement with Texas Monthly Press

PRINTING HISTORY
Texas Monthly Press edition published October 1982
"Riding the Range" copyright © 1982 Louis L'Amour.
Bantam edition/May 1988

Library of Congress Cataloging-in-Publication Data

Schreiber, Martin H.
    Last of a breed.

1. Cowboys—Texas—Pictorial works.   2. Cowboys—Oklahoma—Pictorial works.
3. Cowboys—New Mexico—Pictorial works.   4. Ranch life—Texas—Pictorial works.
5. Ranch life—Oklahoma—Pictorial works.   6. Ranch life—New Mexico—Pictorial
works.   7. Texas—Social life and customs—Pictorial works.   8. Oklahoma—Social life and
customs—Pictorial works.   9. New Mexico—Social life and customs—Pictorial
works.   I. Title.
[F391.2.S29   1988]   976   87-47910
ISBN 0-553-34528-1 (pbk.)

Published simultaneously in the United States and Canada.

Bantam Books are published by Bantam Books, a division of Bantam Dou-
bleday Dell Publishing Group, Inc. Its trademark, consisting of the words
"Bantam Books" and the portrayal of a rooster, is Registered in U.S. Patent
and Trademark Office and in other countries. Marca Registrada.
Bantam Books, 666 Fifth Avenue, New York, New York 10103.

PRINTED IN THE UNITED STATES OF AMERICA
WAK   0   9   8   7   6   5   4   3   2   1

To the patrons I met from Amarillo who made this project possible; may the tradition of the Medici live on.

And to the cowboys I met who made me proud to be a part of this great country; and to their dignity and integrity, may they be an inspiration to us all.

FOREWORD

comment about these photographs, and this book. Photography can never truly convey the qualities, the feelings, inherent in any given subject. If successful, photographs can offer a glimpse into something; if not, they can lie and distort. I have tried with these photographs to give an honest picture, but much of what I felt and saw while working on this project I could never capture with a camera.

In fact, you won't find the most important aspects of the cowboy in my photographs. These are the key qualities that make up the civilized, cultured man, and they are very basic and simple: honesty, integrity, sincerity, kindness. When someone told me he was going to do something, it was done—and never with more of a guarantee than a simple handshake. When I went to the homes of the people I met while working on this project, I was truly welcomed as a member of the family. I have rarely felt so comfortable in the homes of near-strangers.

There exists among these people a genuineness that is exceedingly scarce, a warm hospitality that makes one feel as though one is loved. I point this out because the society that I and so many of us live in is built on false ideals, and I find it frightening. The cowboy, and others like him, stand as guardians of higher values. That is really what this book is about: a testament to man's better qualities and to the ultimate preservation of those qualities. If the photographs point out the obvious romantic facts of the cowboy lifestyle, the essence of these men remains out of view.

The opportunity to live and work with these men, and the photographs that came from my association with them, came by chance. Two years ago I met a group of Texas businessmen and their wives at the Lone Star Cafe in New York, and I asked if I could do their portrait. They came to my studio the next day and enjoyed themselves so much they invited me to visit them in Texas. I left New York the next week and flew all over that enormous state. I visited several ranches, attended a big rodeo, and then turned my attention to the cowboys. Thus, this book.

I began this project a babe in the woods, and soon found myself, at the age of thirty-four, undertaking a serious reexamination of my life. Before I returned to New York, I spent over a year with these people, and in that time the insecurities and suspicions I brought from the East dissipated in the warmth of the friendships I established. I thank all the people who trusted me and had faith, and I thank all the cowboys who made this book.

—M.H.S.
May 26, 1982

Acknowledgments

This book would not have been possible without the support, interest and kindness of each of the following individuals:

Bill Attebury, Mary Miles Batson, Mark Bivens, Ninia Ritchie Bivens, Bobby Boston, Jenks Boston, Mike Campbell, Bettie Childers, Charles Cohen, Joe Conway, Leonard Cornelius, Eugenia Von Gontard, Don Hoffman, Jim Humphries, Monty Johnson, Marta Kramer, Cris Lacy, Jeff Lane, Dave Lane, Winston LeJeune, Sheri Lokey, Wales Madden III, Bob Marrs, Calvin Peters, Montie Ritchie, Josh Russel, Hugh Russel, Hugh Russel Jr., Tommy Wagner, John Wheir, Jim Whittenburg IV, Clark Willingham, Jane Hitch Willingham, and all the cowboys I met and photographed.

RIDING THE RANGE

by Louis L'Amour

These photographs of the contemporary cowboy are the best that I have seen.

To those who believe the cowboy is a creature of myth and imagination, these pictures should be a revelation—for here they are, the working cowboys of today, doing the same things they did yesterday and in much the same manner. Although we have heard lately of something called the "urban cowboy," there is no such thing. The very name is a contradiction in terms, for there is no place in the city for a working cowboy except as a casual visitor.

A cowboy is, literally, a man who works with cows. The saddle is his workbench, designed for the job of working cattle or horses. Wearing boots and a wide-brimmed hat does not make one a cowboy, and no one who has not worked the trade is entitled to the name.

Today, four-wheel-drive vehicles and various forms of aircraft may be used in the handling of stock, but the greater part of the work is done, as always, from the back of a horse. Cattle may not be as wild as they used to be, but occasionally some tough old bull or steer will offer a fight. On one day, a surprised jackrabbit will start cattle running; on another they may pay no attention at all. No cowboy yet has been able to read the mind of a range cow, although a good cow horse may come close. This work is unpredictable, rough, and occasionally dangerous, but if a cowhand has good boots, a good hat, and the right saddle, he couldn't care less about how hard the work is.

One more item is necessary to the care and comfort of a cowhand: a good cook. The outfit with a reputation for having the best cook and the best horses usually had the top hands, and in the old days a good cook might become as well known as a gun-toting marshal or a cowtown madam.

And there is the land—the great, wide open land, a land familiar in all its varied moods, mile upon mile of rolling hill and plain, of rimrock and canyon, of scrub oak and prickly pear, or of piñon and juniper: a land where the cattle graze.

A rider after cattle will soon come to know thousands of acres as a city man knows his desk. The rider will know where the cattle hide, where they go for shade or to escape the flies, where they drink, and where the grass grows green and fresh. He knows the land under the wind, under the rain, under low gray clouds shot with lightning, and under the sun. He will cuss the rain that beats down on his hat and his slicker, and he will cuss the sweat that trickles down his neck, but secretly he loves every bit of it.

Some men are born to the saddle and the high country; others are drawn to it, finding their way as if some inner compass were pointing out the trail. Many of those who come to riding after cattle never leave it; some may go on to other things. But in reality once a man has been a rider, he is always a rider at heart. There will be times when he will lift his eyes from whatever he is doing and look out across the rooftops toward a vision of cattle moving, and in his thoughts he will again have a good horse under him, he will be smelling the dust, feeling the heat of a cattle drive, and looking for the open range.

Hear them dream! Hear the old men talk! Listen to them, their faces sculpted by weather, telling of horses they have ridden and steers they have known, of the rocky trails, the bunkhouses, the line cabins, the corrals. Hear them speak the poetry of brands—the XIT, the Long Rail, the Hashknife, the Running W, the Dogiron, the 101, the L-Open A-K, the R-Bar-T, the Quarter Circle L.

The brands are history, as are the men who rode for them, and when the history of the rangeland is written, it will not be the story of men alone, but of horses and cattle and of particular horses and particular cattle. Stories will be told of steers like Old Blue, who led many a herd over the cattle trails of Texas, Colorado, and Kansas, a belled steer who was worth a half-dozen cowhands and who died when he was twenty. There will be tales of the fabled white mustang who could pace faster than any other horse could run, and who left his stories along the trails from Alberta to Texas. This history will speak of great cutting horses or of outlaw horses no man could ride.

When cowboys get together, they talk of ropers and riders, of horses and cattle; they talk of ranches they have known that are measured by the tens of miles rather than by acres, and of the times they had in towns. They relish every inch of their lives, even though the pay is low and the work is hard. Yet what other job lets a man ride alone under the wide sky or gives a sense of freedom, however illusory, like that which belongs to the cowboy?

Study these pictures well, for these are the cowboys, and this is the work they do and the country in which they do it. They have changed but little. The men in these pictures could have ridden the old trails just as well as their ancestors of long ago.

The Photographs

"I look forward to morning. When I horseback and watch the sun come up and hear the sounds through the stillness it's like God made all of creation just for me, and I think, 'Lord, you sure do pretty work.'"

—*J.W. Beeson*, Saddlemaker
Amarillo, Texas

Foreman, Bell Ranch, New Mexico.

Remuda, Bell Ranch, New Mexico.

Early morning coffee, Bell Ranch, New Mexico.

Jeff Lane, Bell Ranch, New Mexico.

Leo Turner, Bell Ranch, New Mexico.

Bell Ranch, New Mexico.

Bell Ranch, New Mexico.

Jim Eicke, Bell Ranch, New Mexico.

Bell Ranch, New Mexico.

Flanking a calf, Bell Ranch, New Mexico.

End of a long day, Bell Ranch, New Mexico.

Daybreak, Burr Ranch, Eagle Pass, Texas.

Stock, Burr Ranch, Eagle Pass, Texas.

"It gives a man a feeling of freedom to ride—no walls to look at, no traffic jams, and not too many people. To hear spurs and buckles rattling, leather squeaking, horses swishing through dewy grass, horses snorting, gives you a peaceful feeling, a pride that you are here."

—*Ron Cromer*, 6666 Ranch
Panhandle, Texas

6666 Ranch, Panhandle, Texas.

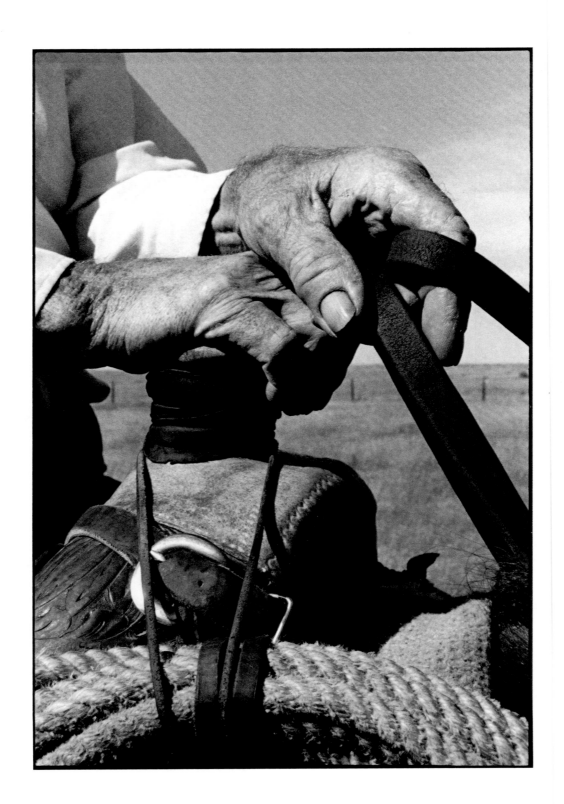

6666 Ranch, Panhandle, Texas.

6666 Ranch, Panhandle, Texas.

Rocky Reagan and Bryan LeJeune at roundup, Burr Ranch, Eagle Pass, Texas.

Esteban, Burr Ranch, Eagle Pass, Texas.

Stock, Quien Sabe Ranch,
Channing, Texas.

Freeze branding, Quien Sabe Ranch, Channing, Texas.

6666 Ranch, Panhandle, Texas.

Bell Ranch, New Mexico.

JA Ranch, Clarendon, Texas.

Montie Ritchie, owner,
JA Ranch, Clarendon, Texas.

"The cattleowner keeps saying we didn't have a very good year this year—maybe next year. Hell, there was bound to have been at least one good year in the last one hundred and fifty."

—*Jim Ray Rentfro*, Quien Sabe Ranch
Channing, Texas

6666 Ranch, Panhandle, Texas.

JA Ranch, Clarendon, Texas.

Ranch hands, Pitchfork Ranch, Guthrie, Texas.

06 Ranch, Alpine, Texas.

Bunkhouse, Pitchfork Ranch, Guthrie, Texas.

Colt, Pitchfork Ranch, Guthrie, Texas.

Foreman, Hitch Ranch, Guymon, Oklahoma.

Chuckwagon, 06 Ranch, Alpine, Texas.

TO Ranch, Raton, New Mexico.

Hitch Ranch, Guymon, Oklahoma.

Wrangler, TO Ranch, Raton, New Mexico.

Day's end, TO Ranch, Raton, New Mexico.

TO Ranch, Raton, New Mexico.

Quien Sabe Ranch, Channing, Texas.

A beer run from the TO Ranch in Raton to Maxwell, New Mexico.

"It is hard to say what a man would like about this part of the country. It is hot, dry, and dusty in the summer; cold, dry, and dustier in the winter. I left it twice, but both places I went were worse."

—Ron Cromer, 6666 Ranch
Panhandle, Texas

Hitch Ranch, Guymon, Oklahoma.

Hitch Ranch, Guymon, Oklahoma.

Hitch Ranch, Guymon, Oklahoma.

Waggoner Ranch, Vernon, Texas.

Line camp, TO Ranch, Raton, New Mexico.

Ranch Hands Rodeo, Wichita Falls, Texas.

Ranch Hands Rodeo, Wichita Falls, Texas.

Bob Brent, Four Way Ranch, Texas.

L. Cornelius Ranch, Bay City, Texas.

Buster Smallwood, Four Way Store, Texas.

Cody, Quien Sabe Ranch,
Channing, Texas.

LS Ranch, Amarillo, Texas.

Stockyards' Cafe, Amarillo, Texas.

Pat's City Bar, Mesquero, New Mexico.

Bob Brent's cattle, Four Way Ranch (South Camp), Texas.

"A lot of boys cowboying today don't remember the days when a nylon rope was a novelty. When I started out grass rope was what was furnished. In the summer they were as limber as a rag, and in winter they were as stiff as a board. If it rained you put them under your slicker; took them to bed with you if you were out with the wagon; and kept them in a lard can when you weren't using them."

—*Ron Cromer,* 6666 Ranch
Panhandle, Texas

Burr Ranch, Eagle Pass, Texas.

06 Ranch, Alpine, Texas.

Bell Ranch, New Mexico.

06 Ranch, Alpine, Texas.

06 Ranch, Alpine, Texas.

Cookhouse, Pitchfork Ranch, Guthrie, Texas.

"Eats," 06 Ranch, Alpine, Texas.

06 Ranch, Alpine, Texas.

Stock pond, 06 Ranch, Alpine, Texas.

Beer run from Quien Sabe Ranch, Channing, Texas.

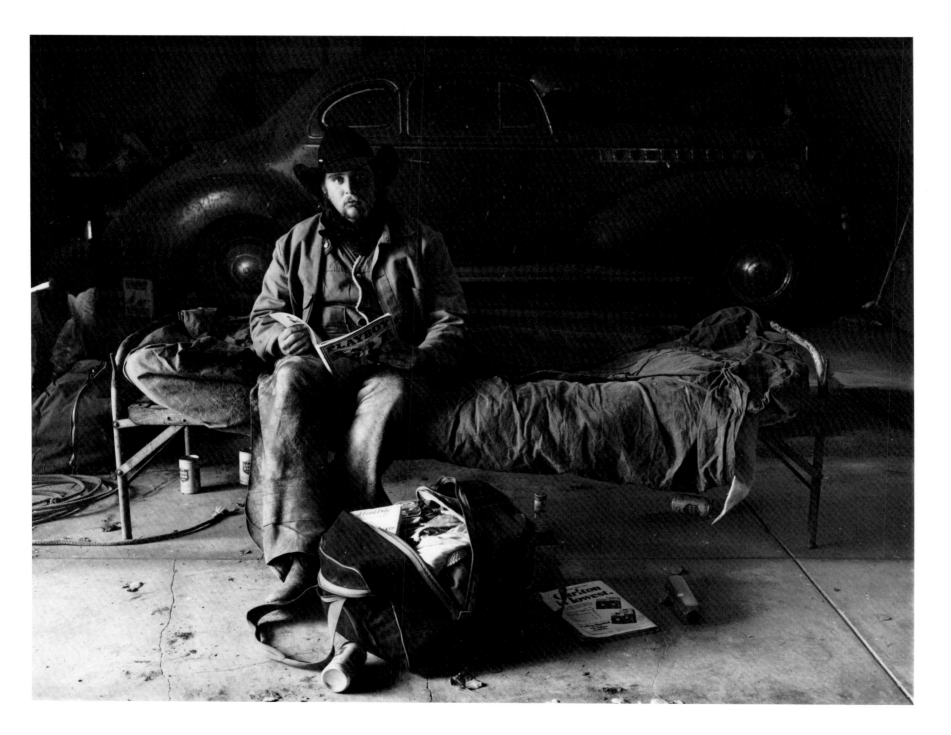

Headquarters' garage, 06 Ranch, Alpine, Texas.

06 Ranch, Alpine, Texas.

06 Ranch, Alpine, Texas.

Stock, Quien Sabe Ranch, Channing, Texas.

J.C. King at Wednesday night roping.

Cowhands, Quien Sabe Ranch, Channing, Texas.

Wedding party, LS Ranch, Amarillo, Texas.

Bride and groom, LS Ranch, Amarillo, Texas.

6666 Ranch, Panhandle, Texas.

"By the time a cowboy gets to be 25 years old he's developed his own look. After that he'll crease his hat the same till he dies."

—Joel Nelson, 06 Ranch
Alpine, Texas

6666 Ranch, Panhandle, Texas.

Quien Sabe Ranch, Channing, Texas.

Quien Sabe Ranch, Channing, Texas.

Quien Sabe Ranch, Channing, Texas.

Branding, Quien Sabe Ranch, Channing, Texas.

06 Ranch, Alpine, Texas.

Quien Sabe Ranch, Channing, Texas.

Dick Shepherd, camp cook, Quien Sabe Ranch, Channing, Texas.

Dick Shepherd's sourdough biscuits,
Quien Sabe Ranch, Channing, Texas.

Quien Sabe Ranch, Channing, Texas.

Cody working cattle, Quien Sabe Ranch, Channing, Texas.

06 Ranch, Alpine, Texas.